Along the Way

Molly Colaneri

Presentation by *BookLeaf Publishing*

Web: www.bookleafpub.com

E-mail: info@bookleafpub.com

ISBN: 9789363306707

First edition 2024

To my children, may you always dream big and find your way.

ACKNOWLEDGEMENT

Thank you to my wonderful family.

Spiderwebs

Unbreakable bonds of family ties wrapped tight
by generations
Over time forming fragile invisible spiderwebs
disappearing in seconds with each gust of death
or marriage
The matriarchal or patriarchal idol and faces of
the family crest slip away leaving tattered pages
of wills and wishes
The family foundation splinters and cracks with
changing relationships and expectations
The dust settles those left clutching what was,
others enter a new unknown with the only
unbreakable bond left being guilt

Hidden Faces

Kept inside you tried to hide
Your face in the mirror
Pretending to be a piece of me
Only to not be a friend
I believed all the lies and oh did I cry
When the truth was untimely revealed
Goodbye to the lie leaving the why
You felt you had to hide

Still

The horizon ahead pulls at my heart
But my comfort keeps me still
I long to be brave and jump
But my fear keeps me still
It's time for something new and bold
But the my inner voice keeps me still
Is my dream on the horizon or is stillness my
path?

Just Jump

Maybe life is the jump the anxious heartbeat the
risk it all rush?
Maybe my dreams are on the edge of my
fingertips if I only close my eyes and reach.
Maybe I live in the stress and panic and the fear
of not being good enough.
Maybe I should….
just…
JUMP

The Goodbye

I don't agree, I can't stay silent, I am not one to smile with empty eyes watching it all burn. But the fight to fix and save and create is too big a price to pay. I am not enough to carry the sword. So with a teary goodbye I watch the embers float and fly. In the quiet charred blackness I find a new home and grow again on my own.

Successful

Measure my title for my time
Measure my perks and pay
Measure my dedication to a 9-5
Measure my late ending day
Measure my decades of loyalty
Measure my silence and say
But does this measure success
Or is there another way?

The Ride

Holding my hand I know I'm safe
But is safe how I want to feel.
The kiss, the rush, the longing of more.
Addicted to the push and pull, tears and
consuming emotions.
Safe I am loved but the thrill of the ride, the
drama of empty promises tugs at me pulling me
towards the coaster. It will be a ride but you will
feel alive riding the track of heartbreak. Jump
in, close your eyes, hold tight. It will be over as
soon as it begins. Back on the ground, legs
unsteady, reaching blindly for the hand that
promises safety.

Fly

You whisper my dreams and tell me to fly. You
make me believe I can do it all.
You bring the wind and push me higher.
You make me believe it's all up to me.
You cradle me gently and give me a landing.
You make me believe I am enough.
I fly to new heights touching the snow capped
peaks.
You are the reason I'm living in the clouds.

Sunshine

When the days feel long and gloomy
When the rain won't stop for days
Your hand gives me hope for sunshine and
rainbows on the way
Your kiss brings the warmth of sunshine
Your embrace pushes away the clouds
Your love promises brilliant sunrises of a
brighter day.

So,

You want a girlfriend but don't want a relationship. You want to go out to dinner but don't want to pay a tip. You won't dedicate your time, your love, yourself, you aren't worth the date.

You want the pay but don't want your work to matter. You want the high office but don't want to climb the ladder. You won't dedicate your time, your love, yourself, you won't get checkmate.

You want to play with your kids but travel all the time. You want to read them stories but fall asleep after booze and lime. You won't dedicate your time, your love, yourself, you aren't worth their wait.

Seconds of Forever

Two seconds to decide the fate of your life.
Two seconds for the words to escape.
Two seconds for every dream to disappear.
Two seconds to slam the door on peace.
Two seconds leaves your heart broken.
Two seconds now picking up pieces forever.

Rolling the Dice

Miles ahead and miles behind of roads to
nowhere. A roll of dice, turn left or right, into
the great unknown wonder. Windows down
breathing in the air of freedom and possibility.
No longer the lead, trees rushing past in a blur,
and only now feeling alive. A roll of dice, turn
left or right, into my new adventure.

Rainbows

I hope you never cry. I hope you're always safe.
I hope you always know your dreams can come
true. I hope you always let me hold you. I hope
I can erase all your pain. I hope you never know
disappointment. I hope you are strong. I hope
you are brave. I hope your heart doesn't break.
I hope you never doubt yourself. I hope you
take risks. I hope you always bet on yourself. I
hope when my fears come true and life leaves
you devastated, you stay you and look for the
rainbows in the storm.

The Storm

My tears created an ocean I drift in looking for land. The darkening of the water and sky blur the lines. Locked in a milky dark marble rolling around with no up or down. Floating with no sound but the teardrops. Upside down and inside out I am lost. I call for help but no one hears or maybe there is no sound. Grief has left me bashing against the waves, floating into the horizon long after the storm.

Stop Signs

I saw the signs and bright red light. I waved my hands to warn my friends but they just walked right by. Closer and closer, I could hear the roar. Louder and louder I made the alarm. Losing friends in the process. Too close to stay, looking down, grabbing arms they pull away, hold my breath and jump. Left alone I wait for more to join. I might be first but not the last. We all have our own stop signs.

Honey

The burn of honey when I expected sweet. The
sting of a flower when I expected soft.
The cut of your smile when I expected gentle
memories.
The heartbreak of moving on when I expected
love.
The pain of you is all that's left when I expected
more.

Sea Salt

The sea salt breeze heals my soul in ways you never could. The warmth of sunshine dries my tears always about you. The soft white sand leaves the same footprint memories you have left in my heart. The salt water waves pull me towards a future apart. The ocean sounds dull my cries searching for reason. I drift away, riding the waves, on the sea salt breeze away from you.

Exit 30

Years of lessons, heartaches and tears. Growing
up with goodbyes and fears.
Motherhood dreams of new life and mirrors.
Titles of woman, mother, wife and dear.
Exit 30 hesitantly looking in rearview mirror.
More heartache or love or fear?
Appreciate the road paved in lessons and shed a
tear.